in·jean·uity

written by **Ellen Warwick** * illustrated by **Bernice Lum**

Kids Can Press

For my mum, Mary — EW

For Susan Harris, who makes the coolest clothes — BL

pLanet girL ™ is a trademark of Kids Can Press Ltd.

Text © 2006 Ellen Warwick
Illustrations © 2006 Bernice Lum

Kids Can Press acknowledges the financial support of the Government of Ontario, through the Ontario Media Development Corporation's Ontario Book Initiative, and the Government of Canada, through the BPIDP, for our publishing activity.

Published in Canada by	Published in the U.S. by
Kids Can Press Ltd.	Kids Can Press Ltd.
29 Birch Avenue	2250 Military Road
Toronto, ON M4V 1E2	Tonawanda, NY 14150

www.kidscanpress.com

Edited by Stacey Roderick
Designed by Karen Powers
Printed and bound in China

CM 06 0 9 8 7 6 5 4 3 2 1

Library and Archives Canada Cataloguing in Publication

Warwick, Ellen
    Injeanuity / written by Ellen Warwick ; illustrated by Bernice Lum.

(Planet girl)
ISBN-13: 978-1-55337-681-1
ISBN-10: 1-55337-681-1

1. Denim — Juvenile literature. 2. Textile crafts — Juvenile literature. I. Lum, Bernice II. Title. III. Series.

TT712.W37 2006   746.9   C2004-906035-X

Kids Can Press is a lorus™ Entertainment company

Contents

HEY JEAN•IUS!

So, you think your jeans are **DULL, DULL, DULL** and there's no other option than to break the bank on some pricey new denim duds? Well, think again 'cause this book is here to rescue you and your wallet.

yawn!

There are heaps of cool, fun and easy projects in here. Fix-ups for **UGLY JEANS**. *Ways to make* **OLD JEANS** *into totally different clothes. Accessories for you, for your room and even for your little sister (if you're feeling nice).*

Inside you'll find everything you'll need to know. Stuff you'll need. **EASY**-*to-follow instructions. Suggestions to make your projects* **UNIQUE**.

Now, reach way back into your closet, pull out all those too-tight, too-short, too-boring jeans and prepare to make **FABULOUS STUFF**. *No old jeans of your own? Ask your family and friends. Or, take a trip down to the local* **THRIFT** *shop, and for a little bit of money get all the jeans you can carry.*

And don't get hung up on trying to make your creations look exactly *like the photos. Think of these projects as your* **INSPIRATION**. *Use them as basic ideas and patterns and then ... use your* **INJEANUITY***!*

STOP!

☞ Did that get your attention?
Good. Do not skip ahead!!
Read this section before you begin!
There's lotsa important information here!

Some Tricks for Working with Denim

⦿ First things first: when choosing jeans to work with, remember that there are tons of styles and cuts out there. But if a project specifically asks for straight-legged jeans, the success of the project will depend on using them. And avoid stretch denim. It can be hard to work with.

⦿ Make sure you wash and dry your jeans before working with them. Always wash jeans inside out after adding any trims or decorations so all your hard work doesn't get damaged by the washing machine.

⦿ Most projects will look a little neater if you iron the seams flat and open as you work through the steps or when you're finished. But always ask permission to use the iron and please — be careful!

⦿ Ever heard of Fray-Stop? It's amazing stuff. You can get it at any fabric or craft store. Just squeeze a little of this clear goop on the cut edges of denim. Once it dries, the edges won't unravel or fray.

⦿ And remember, one pair of jeans can make many things. After you've liberated a leg or a pocket or two for one project, save the rest. There's lots of other stuff to make, too!

SEAMS

For some projects you'll need to split jean seams open. So what's there to know?

regular seam

Some seams are just the regular kind: two pieces of fabric sewn together with one line of stitching. But jeans also have flat-felled seams. These seams are folded over a couple times and sewn with two lines of stitching. They're much harder to split open than regular seams. So do yourself a favor and open regular seams whenever possible.

flat-felled seam

How? Easy! Start at one end of the seam and break open the stitches using scissors or a stitch ripper. A stitch ripper — sometimes called a seam ripper — is a special tool just for opening stitches. It's a little faster and a lot easier than using scissors. You can buy one very cheaply at a sewing supply store or a discount store. Once you're done, pull out the little bits of broken thread.

Sewing: Stuff You Should Know

⦿ Before you pick up scissors or a needle, read all the instructions for the project to make sure you get it. It'll be super irritating if you get partway through a project and get stuck.

⦿ Here's a little thing but an important one: When you pin fabric together for sewing, the pins should be at a right angle to the fabric edge.

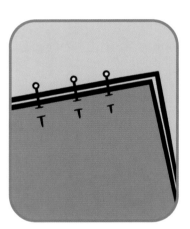

This is especially crucial when you're using a sewing machine. Otherwise the pins will get caught in the machine and mess up everything. Make sure you remove the pins as you sew.

⦿ Because denim is such a heavy fabric, you'll need to use sturdy thread and a heavy needle that's made for sewing denim.

⦿ Making a few extra stitches at the corners and the beginning and end of your stitching will reinforce your sewing. If you're using a sewing machine, sew almost to the end of the seam, backstitch a few stitches, and then forward again to the end.

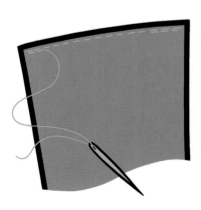

HAND SEWING VS. SEWING MACHINES

◉ We'd love to tell you it's as easy to sew these projects by hand, but a machine is much easier and faster for seams and hems, especially with heavier material like denim.
(*We used a needle and thread in the illustrations to show you which direction to sew in.)

◉ Freaking out at the thought of using a sewing machine? All you need to know for this book is how to thread the machine and how to stitch forward and backward. Easy! If you haven't had much experience using a sewing machine, ask someone to show you how. (The owner's manual can help you, too.) Practicing on a scrap of denim first will also help.

◉ Here's a tip: if you're sewing a different color fabric onto the denim, thread the machine so the top thread matches the fabric and the bottom thread is dark blue to match the jeans. This way the stitches won't show on either side.

◉ If you do any sewing by hand, make close, even stitches and definitely use a thimble! It'll save your fingers from the pain of pushing a needle through thick layers of fabric.

9

TRACING PAPERS

Tracing paper and dressmaker's tracing paper are not the same stuff. Tracing paper is thin paper you can see through to trace a design. Dressmaker's tracing paper is thicker and has colored ink on one side.

To use dressmaker's tracing paper, place the colored side down on your fabric. Pressing firmly with a pencil or pen, draw your design on top. The design will magically be transferred onto the fabric. And don't worry — it washes off just as magically.

SEAMS VS. HEMS

What's the diff? A seam is made when two pieces of fabric are sewn together. A hem is the finished edge of a piece of fabric. To make a hem, fold the fabric under, pin and sew in place.

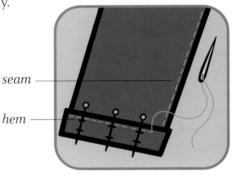

seam

hem

When a measurement is given for a seam or a hem, it means the width from the edge of the material to the line of sewing. Most sewing machines have seam guidelines to help you keep your seams the right width.

RSF, WSF, RSTOG, WSTOG

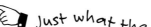 Just what the heck do these mean?

RSF = Right side facing.
The right side, or good side
of the material, faces you.

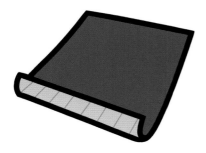

WSF = Wrong side facing.
The wrong side, or underside
of the material, faces you.

RSTOG = Right sides together.
The right sides of two pieces of
material are placed together.

WSTOG = Wrong sides together.
The wrong sides of two pieces of
material are placed together.

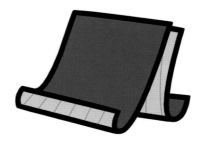

EMBROIDERY

Isn't embroidery just sewing? It is in a way because you use simple hand-sewing stitches for these projects. The difference is that these stitches are decorative and aren't always in a straight line. Think of embroidery as an excellent way to customize your projects!

Use an embroidery needle, which is just like a big sewing needle. Most embroidery thread is made up of six strands wound together to make one thick thread. You can separate the strands and use just one or two at a time, but we used all six strands together for bolder designs. For each color you use, thread your needle with a knotted thread. When you're finished, tie a knot close to the wrong side of the material and cut off the extra thread.

⦿ For the Summer Cuffs on page 19, we just used simple stitches of different lengths. You can lightly draw your design on first, or do what we did and just wing it!

1. Poke the threaded needle up through the fabric, and pull the thread through until the knot catches. (The knot should be on the side of the material that won't be seen.)

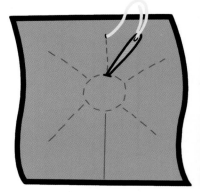

2. Following the pattern, push the needle back down through the fabric. Don't make stitches longer than 5 to 8 cm (2 to 3 in.) or they will be too loose.

3. Pull the thread all the way through, but don't pull it too tight. The stitch should lie flat without making the fabric bunch up.

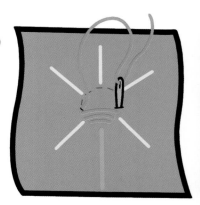

4. Keep going until you're done or want to change the color of your thread.

⊙ For the Oh-So-Sweet Slippers on page 48, we used an overcast stitch. It's easy.

1. Pull the threaded needle up through the fabric, right beside the cut-out appliqué.

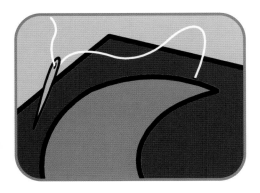

2. Push the needle down into the appliqué, about 0.5 cm (¼ in.) over. Pull the thread all the way through.

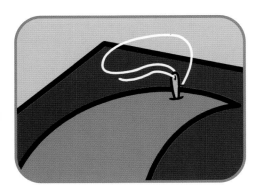

3. Bring the needle back up again, right beside the appliqué and about 0.5 cm (¼ in.) from the previous stitch.

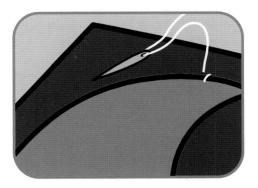

4. Continue sewing around the appliqué until your stitches meet.

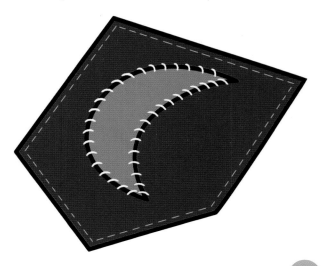

Some Details about Denim

◉ Where does the word "denim" come from? Probably from the French **SERGE DE NÎMES**, which means fabric (serge) from Nîmes (a town in France where it was originally made).

◉ Get this! The actress **MARLENE DIETRICH** shocked the world when she wore pants in public in 1932. Why? Because before that women and girls were not supposed to wear pants in public.

◉ The **MOST POPULAR** type of clothing in the world hasn't always been called "jeans." Dungarees, overalls, waist overalls, blue jeans or denims are some of the other names they've been called over the years. Wonder what they'll be called in the future?

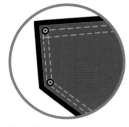

◉ **LEVI STRAUSS** was the creator of jeans as we know them. The first pair that look like the kind we wear today were made way back in 1873. There were pants made of denim before Levi came along, but he was the first to add metal rivets to jeans to make them super strong for workers.

◉ Up until the 1950s, jeans were strictly boring **WORKWEAR**. Then jeans became almost a uniform for young people. Kids of the 1950s were known as "the generation born in blue."

◉ In the 1950s, parents and schools were so worried that wearing jeans was turning kids into **HOOLIGANS**, jeans were banned in some schools!

Cuffs 'N' Stuff

☞ OKAY, this section is perfect for you if any of these SOUND FAMILIAR:

☐ *Your jeans still fit and they look all right, but you're BORED sick of them. You want something — anything — different.*

☐ *You saw an amazing pair of jeans at the mall, but they cost as much as a new TV! You know you can make them for WAAAAAAAY LESS money.*

☐ *You went to school in your new jeans and everyone had the same pair (including your science teacher — gag). You don't want to be a CLONE.*

☐ *Your favorite jeans still look great at the top, but they're riding above your ankles because of a recent GROWTH SPURT.*

Flippin' fantastic cuffs

Flip 'em down in the winter.
Flip 'em up in the summer.
Either way, you'll flip over
these all-weather jeans.

STUFF YOU NEED

- a pair of jeans you still wear
- tracing paper
- dressmaker's tracing paper
- an embroidery needle and embroidery thread in white, green and at least three bright colors
- 0.5 m ($1/_2$ yd.) of blue fabric for cuffs
- thread to match the fabric and jeans
- scissors, pins, a measuring tape, a pencil

Plan B: Decorate the inside and outside of your cuffs with designs that work ALL YEAR ROUND.

For the winter side:

✳ *Note: you'll find snowflake templates on the inside back cover.*

1 Lay the jeans flat and measure 10 cm (4 in.) up from the hem of each leg. Draw a faint line from side seam to side seam. This is the area you'll decorate.

2 Trace the snowflakes from the inside back cover onto the tracing paper. Cut out the snowflakes, leaving about 2.5 cm (1 in.) around them.

3 Place one of the snowflakes on top of the dressmaker's tracing paper. Trace the snowflake onto the bottom section of one leg of the jeans (see page 10). Repeat as many times as you like, using all the snowflake patterns to decorate all around the leg.

4 Using white embroidery thread, embroider over the snowflake designs (see page 12).

5 Repeat steps 3 and 4 all around the other leg.

For the summer side:

1 Measure the hem of one leg from seam to seam. Double this measurement and add another 2.5 cm (1 in.). Mark and cut a piece of fabric this length by 13 cm (5 in.) wide.

2 Fold both long edges of the fabric over 1 cm (½ in.) and pin.

3 With the needle and green embroidery thread, sew some stems using short and long stitches. Then, using different colors, stitch the petals on the stem tops. Last, fill in the centers of the flowers with other colors using small, close stitches. Make sure all the thread knots are on the back of the fabric. If you want, draw your design first with a pencil and then embroider over it. (Check out page 12 for more help if you need it.)

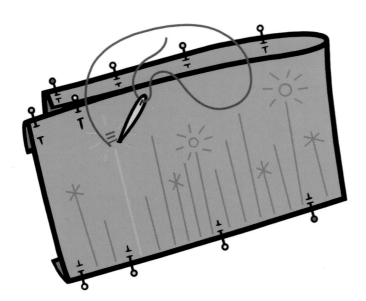

4 Turn the jeans inside out (winter side in). With the flowers right side out and upside down, start at the inner leg seam and pin the fabric to the bottom of the jean leg. Where the fabric ends meet, tuck each under 2.5 cm (1 in.) and pin them.

5 Sew the fabric in place along the pinned edges with a 0.5 cm (¼ in.) seam.

6 Repeat steps 1 to 5 for the other leg. Turn the jeans right side out and fold up the cuffs to show the flowers. Good-bye snow — hello sunshine!

Swell bells

- a pair of jeans with regular seams on the outside
- 1 m (1 yd.) of fabric
- thread to match the fabric and jeans
- scissors, a stitch ripper, pins, a measuring tape
- an iron and an ironing board

Don't worry about going out and spending your hard-earned money on brand new fabric. You can make these bell-bottoms using an old concert T-shirt or something else unusual from your closet or the thrift store.

1 Cut two pieces of fabric 35 cm x 18 cm (14 in. x 7 in.).

2 Measure and mark 30 cm (12 in.) up the outer seam from the hem of each jean leg. Open the outer seams up to the marks.

20

For something SIMPLER,
forget the cuff and
HEM the fabric insert
the SAME LENGTH
as the jeans.

21

3 Working on one leg at a time, place one piece of fabric from step 1 inside the leg RSF. Make a **V** with the cut seam that is 13 cm (5 in.) wide across the bottom. Pin the fabric into the **V**, making sure there are at least 2.5 cm (1 in.) of extra fabric around all three sides.

5 Repeat steps 2 to 4 on the other leg. Trim any excess fabric along the new seams, leaving at least 1 cm (1/2 in.) extra. Iron all new seams flat.

4 Turn the leg inside out. Sew the fabric in place by stitching up each side of the split seam, making a few extra stitches across the top of the triangle.

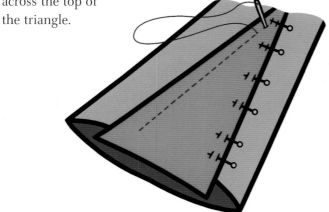

6 For the cuffs, turn the jeans right side out. Lay one leg flat and measure the new width across the hem. Double this measurement and add another 2.5 cm (1 in.). Mark and cut two pieces of fabric this length and 18 cm (7 in.) wide.

7 Fold the long edges of both pieces of fabric over 2.5 cm (1 in.) and pin them. Carefully iron the folds flat and remove the pins. Fold both pieces in half lengthwise WSTOG and iron them flat.

8 Working on one leg at a time and starting at the inner seam, insert the bottom of a jean leg into the cuff so the hem fits into the cuff's center fold. Pin the cuff in place all the way around. Fold one open end of the cuff under 2.5 cm (1 in.) to make a neat finish and pin in place.

9 Using matching thread, sew the cuff in place 1 cm (¹/₂ in.) from its top edge. Then, sew the seam where the cuff ends meet. Remove the pins.

10 Repeat steps 8 and 9 for the other leg. Now these are some jeans with flare!

Jean Gem:

If your favorite jeans are ready for a flood (too short!), add some length when you add the cuffs in steps 8 and 9. Insert the jeans only partway into the cuff, making sure you have at least 1 cm (½ in.) overlap to sew the cuff on. You can add about 6 cm (2¼ in.) of length this way.

Side-splitting fun

Here's a fix if you just can't squeeze your best jeans on anymore (ugh! too snug!). And don't buy the fabric if you have other plans for your precious cash — any found fabric will work.

- a pair of too-small jeans
- 1 m (1 yd.) of fabric
- thread to match the jeans
- scissors, a stitch ripper, pins, a measuring tape

1 The best way to tackle this project is to work on one leg at a time. Split the entire outer seam open. Cut open the waistband above the split seam.

2 Measure the length of the jeans from top to bottom and add another 5 cm (2 in.). Mark and cut an 8 cm (3 in.) wide strip of fabric this size for each leg. (You may need to cut two strips and sew them together to make one long enough.)

FYI: This works best with jeans that have REGULAR SEAMS on the outside.

25

3 Fold over one short end of the fabric strip 1 cm (¹/₂ in.) and pin it. Sew the edge and remove the pins.

4 Turn the jeans inside out. Lining up the sewn edge of the fabric strip with the top of the waistband, pin the strip all the way down one side of the open leg. The fabric and jean should make a 1 cm (¹/₂ in.) seam.

5 Sew this seam in place, making extra stitches at the waist. Remove the pins.

6 Repeat steps 4 and 5 with the other side of the fabric to finish the leg.

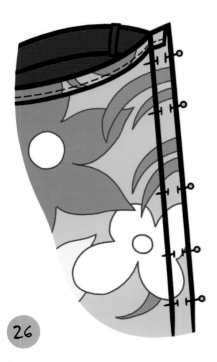

7 Fold and pin the bottom of the fabric strip under so it is even with the hem of the jeans. Sew in place. Remove the pins and trim any excess fabric, leaving at least 1 cm (¹/₂ in.).

Jean Gem:

Wanna have even more fun? Instead of ordinary fabric, try wide satiny ribbons, washable faux suede or fun fur. Or, split the difference and sew together long patchwork strips of small pieces of different material.

8 Repeat steps 1 to 7 for the other leg. Turn the jeans right side out and you're ready to party!

Waistband wonderland

STUFF YOU NEED

- a pair of jeans you still wear
- a package of blanket binding
- thread to match the blanket binding
- 4 m (4 yd.) of thin cord
- a large darning needle or a safety pin
- a few beads
- scissors, a stitch ripper, pins, a measuring tape

This finish is so funky and so simple you'll be tempted to do this to all of your jeans. And think how cute this would look on a jean skirt, too!

1 Open the fly of the jeans and leave it open until the project is finished.

2 Using the stitch ripper, remove the waistband and belt loops.

3 Measure the length of the removed waistband and add 2.5 cm (1 in.). Cut a piece of blanket binding this size. Cut another piece of blanket binding 10 cm (4 in.) long.

Take it a step further: Add matching binding to the cuffs, too (see steps 8 to 10 in Swell Bells).

And use some extra beads and cord to make yourself a matching necklace or bracelet.

4 Fold a short edge of the longer piece of binding under 2.5 cm (1 in.) and pin it.

5 Starting with the folded edge, pin the binding around the waist to make your new waistband. Make sure you begin where the flap overlaps the zipper and that the waist of the jeans is tucked about 1 cm ($\frac{1}{2}$ in.) inside the binding.

6 About 5 cm (2 in.) from the end of the waist (just before the zipper), fold the binding under 2.5 cm (1 in.) and pin it.

7 To make a slot for the cord to be strung through and to complete the waistband, slide the shorter piece of binding 2.5 cm (1 in.) inside the longer piece. Pin the shorter piece along the waist, folding the end 2.5 cm (1 in.) under.

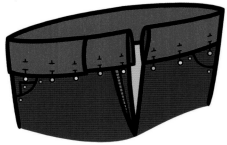

8 Sew the binding in place using a 0.5 cm ($\frac{1}{4}$ in.) seam. Starting where the flap overlaps the zipper, begin stitching 1 cm ($\frac{1}{2}$ in.) down from the top edge and sew all the way around the waist. Sew right up to the top of the binding.

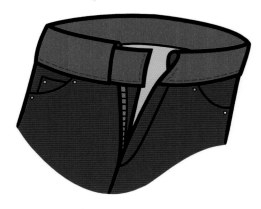

9 Sew the two pieces of binding together where they meet, leaving a 1 cm (1/2 in.) space at the top.

10 Cut the cord into three equal pieces. Using the large darning needle or the safety pin, thread each piece of cord through the open holes in the blanket binding edge. Trim the cords if they are too long for you.

11 Thread beads onto each of the cord ends and tie a knot at the end of each one. Tied tight to fit your waist or loose to hang more on your hips, don't ya love these?

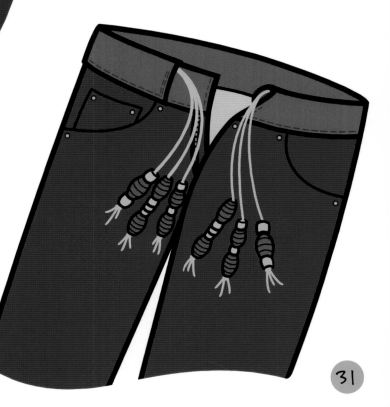

Crazy cuffs

- a pair of jeans you still wear
- ribbons or other trims
- thread to match the ribbons and trims
- scissors, pins, a measuring tape

There's no limit to how many (or few) ribbons and trims you can use for these fancy cuffs. Don't bother trying to find the exact trims we used — it'll be impossible. Instead, create your own look.

1 Lay your collection of ribbons or trims on a jean cuff and experiment with placing and spacing them until you love the look.

2 Measure the hem of a leg from seam to seam. Double this measurement and add another 2.5 cm (1 in.). Cut the ribbons or trims this length.

32

WHO says BOTH legs

have to MATCH?

3 Start at the inner seam and pin a piece of ribbon or trim around the hem. When you get back around to the starting point, tuck one end of the ribbon or trim under itself and pin it in place.

4 Sew the ribbon or trim in place along its top edge, making sure to sew a few extra stitches on the overlapped ends.

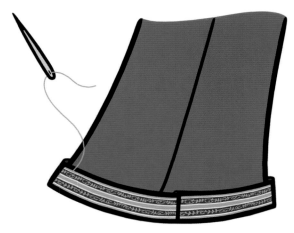

5 Repeat steps 3 and 4 using the rest of the ribbons or trim.

6 Repeat steps 1 to 5 for the other leg.

Jean Gem:

Don't stop now! Why not try this look on jean skirts, shorts or even the cuffs and collar of a jean jacket? Or along the edges of pockets? Or how about skipping the ribbons and customizing your cuffs with a collection of buttons, beads or plastic jewels? Or ... well, the possibilities are endless!

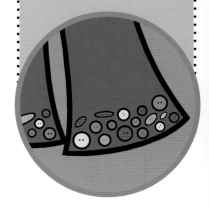

NEW threads from OLD duds

👉 You're in the RIGHT SECTION if any of these appeal to your INNER JEANIUS:

☐ *Morphing jeans that no amount of beads, bobbles or trim can possibly improve into something* **FABULOUS**

☐ *Making* **NEW CLOTHES** *materialize without going shopping (and without spending lots of cash!)*

☐ *Creating new life out of old jeans while helping the* **ENVIRONMENT** *by not adding to landfills*

☐ *All of the above —* **WHY STOP** *at one?*

Wrap 'n' go skirt

Wrap up your wardrobe with this skirt made of old jeans. Make it simple and pretty with just a little ribbon trim or doll it up with some fringe, studs or even a fancy pin. This one is short and sassy, but yours could be super mini, midi or even ankle length.

STUFF YOU NEED

- 2 pairs of wide, straight-legged jeans
- 30 cm (12 in.) of 2.5 cm (1 in.) self-adhesive Velcro
- 2 m (2 yd.) of 2.5 cm (1 in.) wide ribbon and matching thread
- thread to match the jeans
- scissors, a stitch ripper, pins, a measuring tape, a pencil

1 Decide how long you want your skirt to be. Measure from your waist down to this point and add another 5 cm (2 in.). Measuring up from the hem, mark and cut three jean legs this length. Open one side seam of each leg to make three panels of denim.

36

The ADJUSTABLE waist means it will FIT you ...

and your FRIENDS who borrow it!

2 Measure around your hips and add 35 cm (14 in.). This is the width of fabric you'll need. Lay the jean panels out flat, side by side, and measure across to make sure you have enough fabric. Use a fourth jean leg if you need more fabric. Or if you have too much, trim one panel down for the correct width.

3 Pin two panels RSTOG along the opened seams. Sew a 1 cm (1/2 in.) seam down the length. Repeat to attach the third panel (and fourth, if necessary) so the panels make one big piece. Remove the pins.

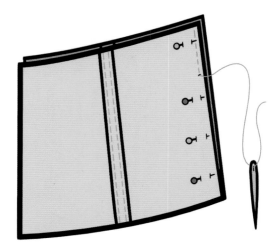

4 Pin and sew a 1 cm (1/2 in.) hem down the two short sides. Remove the pins.

5 Pin and sew a 2.5 cm (1 in.) hem along the top and bottom of the skirt. Remove the pins.

6 Lay the skirt down WSF. Separate the Velcro into two pieces. Stick one piece along the top edge, starting at the top left corner.

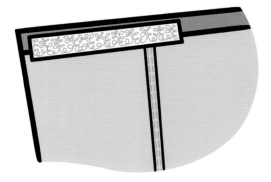

7 Turn the skirt over and lay it down RSF. Stick the other Velcro piece in place as in step 6.

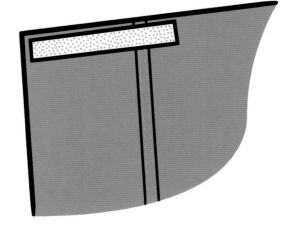

8 Sew around the edges of both Velcro pieces.

9 Measure around the bottom and cut ribbon this length. Repeat for both side edges. Pin and sew the ribbons in place using matching thread. Remove the pins. Now, wrap your skirt around you and go, go, go!

Hot daze halter

Beat the heat with this feisty halter top, or wear it all year round over a fitted T-shirt. Either way, you'll knock 'em dead.

- 1 leg from a pair of jeans
- 5 m (5 yd.) of 0.5 cm (1/4 in.) wide ribbon
- 0.5 m (1/2 yd.) of 1 cm (1/2 in.) wide ribbon
- thread to match the jeans
- scissors, a stitch ripper, pins, a measuring tape, a pencil

1 Open the regular seam of the jean leg and lay it flat.

2 Measure 30 cm (12 in.) up the center (flat-felled) seam from the bottom hem. Make a pencil mark here. Measure and mark 17 cm (6 1/2 in.) across from this mark on both sides of the seam. Join these three points with a straight line.

3 Across the bottom hem, measure and mark 22 cm (8 1/2 in.) on each side of the center seam. Connect the lines as shown. Cut along the three drawn lines.

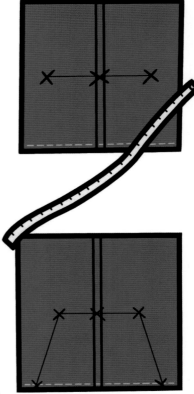

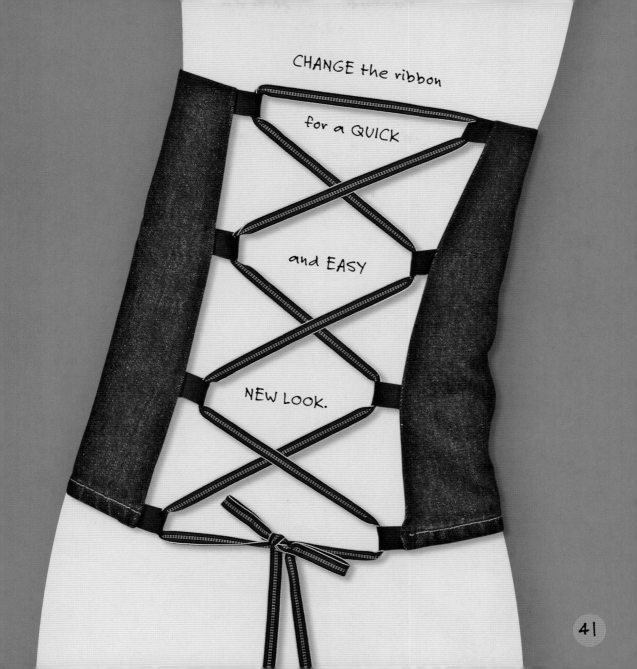

CHANGE the ribbon

for a QUICK

and EASY

NEW LOOK.

4 With WSF, fold and pin a 1 cm (¹/₂ in.) hem all the way around the three cut edges. Sew the hem and remove the pins.

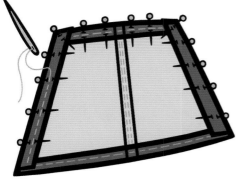

5 Cut eight 5 cm (2 in.) pieces of the 1 cm (¹/₂ in.) ribbon.

6 For each corner, make a loop by folding a piece of ribbon in half and pinning it in place. Make sure that the loop is just large enough for the long ribbon to fit through. Sew the loop ends securely and remove the pins.

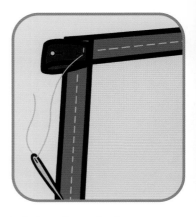

7 Measure and mark 10 cm (4 in.) up from the bottom corners. Measure and mark 10 cm (4 in.) down from the top two corners. Repeat step 6 to sew ribbon loops for each mark.

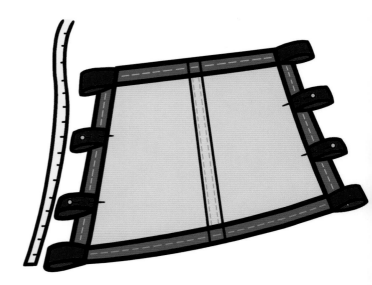

8 Cut the ends of the 0.5 cm (1/4 in.) ribbon at an angle to prevent fraying. Starting at the top, thread the ribbon through the two corner loops so the ends are even. Lace the ribbon through the remaining loops in a crisscross pattern like you would a shoelace.

9 To wear your halter, pull it on over your head and shoulders so it ties at the back of your torso. Pull the ribbon ends tight and use a double knotted bow. (You wouldn't want the bow to come undone!) Trim the ends if you find them too long.

Flirty skirt convert

STUFF YOU NEED

- a pair of jeans
- thread to match the jeans
- scissors, pins, a measuring tape, a pencil

Friday you wore those hideous jeans for the last time. By Monday, they'll be a sassy new skirt. Guess what you're making this weekend?

1 Put the jeans on and measure from the waistband down to where you want the skirt to end. Add another 5 cm (2 in.). Take the jeans off.

2 Lay the jeans flat, and measure and mark the length from step 1 down each leg. Draw a straight line across. Cut off the legs along this line.

3 Cut along the back edge of the inside leg seam up to the crotch. Cut the front seam open up to the fly. Cut the back seam open up to the end of the curve.

4 Lay the skirt flat, front side up. Place the flap so it overlaps to the left and pin it. Sew it in place and remove the pins. Repeat this step for the back.

MIX it up and use a funky FABRIC ...

or CORDUROY instead of the jean panel in step 5.

5 Lay the skirt front side up again. Cut a piece from one of the cut-off legs that's larger than the V opening. Pin the panel inside the V and sew it in place with a 0.5 cm (¹/₄ in.) seam. (You can turn under the V edges before sewing for a more finished look.) Remove the pins.

6 Turn the skirt over and repeat step 5 for the back.

7 Turn the skirt inside out and trim any excess fabric from along the V edges and the flaps that are not sewn, leaving 2.5 cm (1 in.) of extra fabric all around.

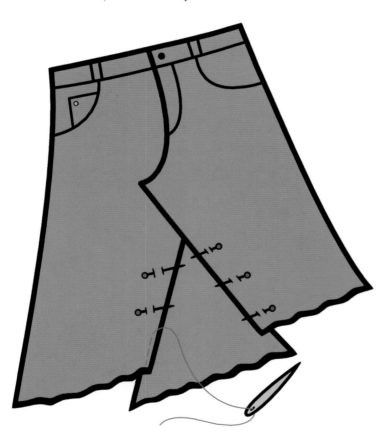

8 Lay the skirt flat and trim the bottom so it is even. or you can cut the bottom of the skirt so it is asymmetrical, or uneven, if you like. An unfinished bottom will fray as you wash it for a funky look. Or you can hem it for a neater finish.

In·jean·ius Accessories

☞ keep turning the pages if you want to TRANSFORM your DULLEST denims into any of the following FASHIONABLE and functional ACCESSORIES:

- ☐ *Slippers that PROTECT your tender toes around the house*

- ☐ *A purse to CARRY your essentials and a great bag to HAUL your gear*

- ☐ *A wallet to STASH your cash*

- ☐ *A kerchief to TAME unruly hair*

- ☐ *Wristbands that look COOLER than any precious jewelry*

Oh-so-sweet slippers

Tuck your tootsies into these toasty pockets and slip into slipper heaven. And don't forget step 10 or you may find yourself slipping right onto your behind!

✱ *Note: you'll find star and moon templates on the inside back cover.*

1 First (and this is very important), slide your feet into the back pockets of the jeans. The pockets should fit your feet the way slippers would. Neatly cut the pockets off and trim any extra fabric from the inside.

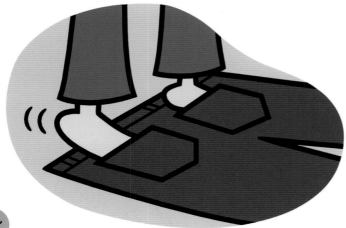

STUFF YOU NEED

- a pair of jeans • tracing paper
- felt • fabric glue
- embroidery needle and embroidery thread
- 0.5 m (1/2 yd.) of 1 cm (1/2 in.) thick foam
- Fray-Stop • puffy fabric paint
- thread to match the jeans
- scissors, pins, a measuring tape, a pencil

2 Trace the star and moon shapes from the back flap onto tracing paper and cut them out. Trace the shapes onto the felt and cut them out. Glue one shape onto each pocket RSF and allow to dry.

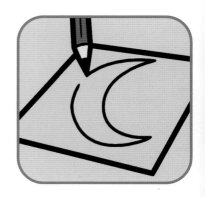

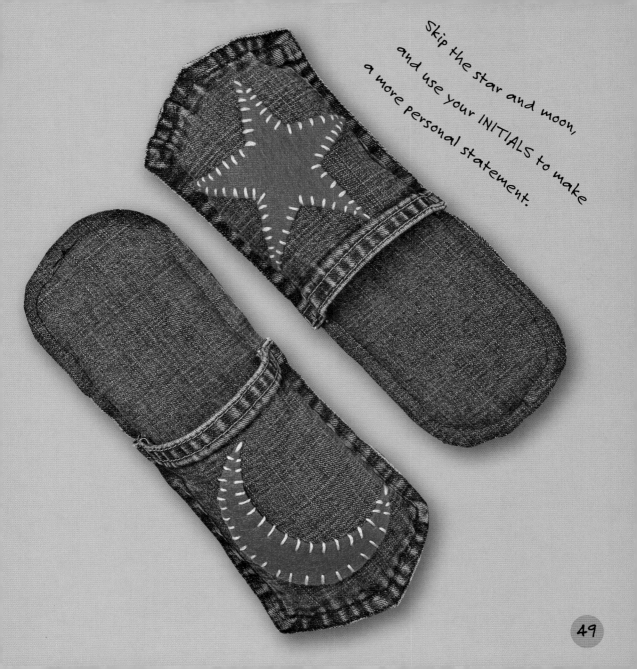

Skip the star and moon, and use your INITIALS to make a more personal statement.

3 Using several strands of embroidery thread, sew around each shape with an overcast stitch (see page 13).

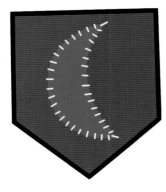

4 Measure the length of the bottom of your foot and add 2.5 cm (1 in.). Measure the width of the bottom of your foot and add 2.5 cm (1 in.). Using these measurements, draw a rectangle on tracing paper. Cut it out and round off the corners. This is your pattern for the soles of the slippers.

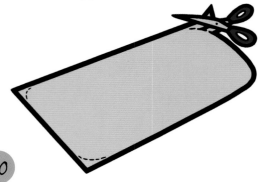

5 To make the soles, trace around the pattern twice onto the foam and four times onto some denim from the jeans. Cut these pieces out.

6 Sandwich a piece of foam between two pieces of denim, WSTOG. Pin the pieces together. Repeat with the other pieces.

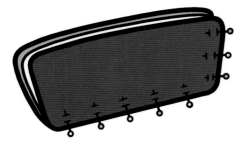

7 Lay one pocket on each sole so the bottom of the pocket is at the top of the sole. Pin the pockets to the soles, lining up the outside edges as neatly as you can.

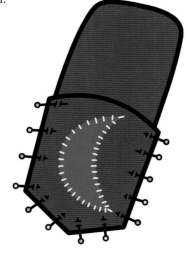

8 Sew around the outside edge of each slipper, 1 cm (¹/₂ in.) in from the edge. Remove the pins.

9 Apply Fray-Stop to the denim edges of the soles.

10 Using puffy paint, draw squiggly lines on the bottom of each slipper to make them nonslip. Allow to dry. Cozy and cute!

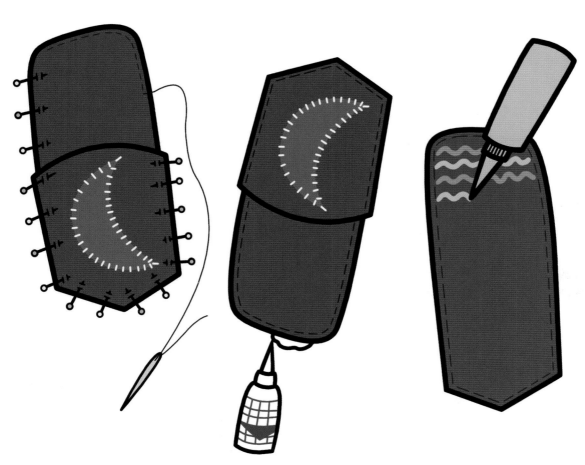

Punky pocket purse

This purse is big enough to hold your essentials, stylish enough for a party and unique enough to turn heads.

STUFF YOU NEED

- 2 back pockets from a pair of jeans
- 38 cm (15 in.) of bead chain with couplings (from a hardware store)
- 2 chicago bolts, $8/32$ x $1/4$ (from a hardware, office supply or craft store)
- 40 cm (16 in.) of elastic cord
- 2 small metal nuts
- thread to match the jeans
- scissors, pins, a measuring tape

1 Neatly trim off any extra fabric from the inside and around the edge of the pockets.

2 Place the pockets WSTOG and pin. Leaving the top open, sew around the pocket edges. Remove the pins.

Make this bag for a friend ...

and tuck a little present inside for two gifts in one!

53

3 For the handle, attach a coupling to each end of the chain. Cut two 4 cm (1½ in.) pieces of elastic cord. Thread a piece of cord through each coupling. Fold the cords in half, and pin the ends of the cords between the outer edges of the pockets about 2.5 cm (1 in.) from the top. Hand sew the cords securely in place. Remove the pins.

4 Measure and mark the center of one side of the purse, about 2.5 cm (1 in.) below the top opening. Poke a small hole into the mark and fasten a chicago bolt through the hole with the longer side on the outside. Repeat on the other side of the purse.

5 Fold the rest of the elastic cord in half and make a knot about 1 cm (1/2 in.) from the fold. Slip the loop over one chicago bolt and pull the knot tight to secure it.

6 Fold the cord ends over to the other side of the purse and tie a knot under the other chicago bolt. Slip a metal nut onto each cord end and secure with a knot. Nutty!

Jean Gem:

Turn punky into pretty by using ribbon for the handle and closure, replacing the chicago bolts with buttons and embroidering the purse with delicate flowers.

Cool carry-all

Carry your gear around in super style. Make a statement by decorating it, or leave it simple and sophisticated.

1 Lay the jeans flat. Measure and mark 34 cm (13 1/2 in.) up from the bottom hem of each leg. Draw a straight line across each leg. Cut off both legs along this line.

2 Open the regular side seams of each leg and remove any extra thread bits.

3 Measure the width of the placemat and the width of the jean legs. If needed, trim the jean legs so they are 2.5 cm (1 in.) wider than the placemat, on each side centering the flat-felled seams.

Make a place to hook your KEYS
by liberating a BELT LOOP from the jeans ...

and sewing it inside the bag.

4 Lay the pieces RSTOG with the hemmed edges together. Pin around three sides, leaving the hemmed edges open.

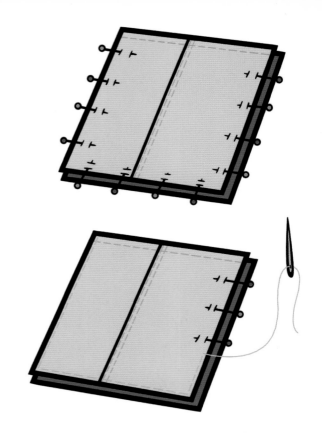

5 Sew a 1 cm (1/2 in.) seam around the pinned edges. Sew over this line of stitching again for strength. Remove the pins and turn the bag right side out.

6 Lay the bag flat and insert the placemat WSF about 15 cm (6 in.) below the opening. Pin to one side of the bag.

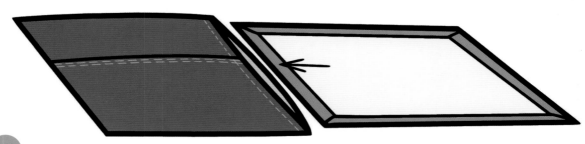

7 Sew a 1 cm (1/2 in.) seam across the opening of the bag to secure the placemat. Remove the pins.

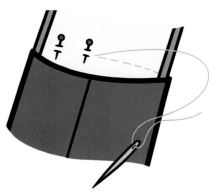

8 Fold under one end of the strap 5 cm (2 in.). Pin it to one side of the bag 5 cm (2 in.) below the top edge. Sew it in place like this:

9 Try on the bag and mark how long you want the strap to be. Add 5 cm (2 in.) and cut off any extra strapping. Repeat step 8 on the other side of the bag. Now you're ready to load it up. This bag can take it!

Wicked wallet

Put whatever you like in the clear outside pockets of this snappy wallet — pics of your friends, concert tixs, whatever!

STUFF YOU NEED

- a leg from a pair of jeans
- 20 cm x 20 cm (8 in. x 8 in.) of clear plastic (from a fabric store)
- 10 cm (4 in.) of 2.5 cm (1 in.) self-adhesive Velcro
- 50 cm (20 in.) of 2.5 cm (1 in.) red grosgrain ribbon or other sturdy trim
- red thread
- masking tape
- scissors, pins, a measuring tape, a pencil, a ruler

1 Starting at the bottom hem of the leg, measure and mark a rectangle that is 20 cm (8 in.) wide and 23 cm (9 in.) high. Cut it out.

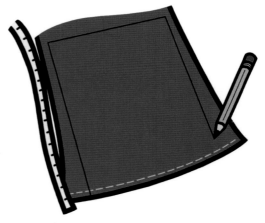

2 Lay the denim down RSF and place the plastic on top, 0.5 cm (1/4 in.) up from the hem edge. Use a few pieces of masking tape to hold the plastic in place.

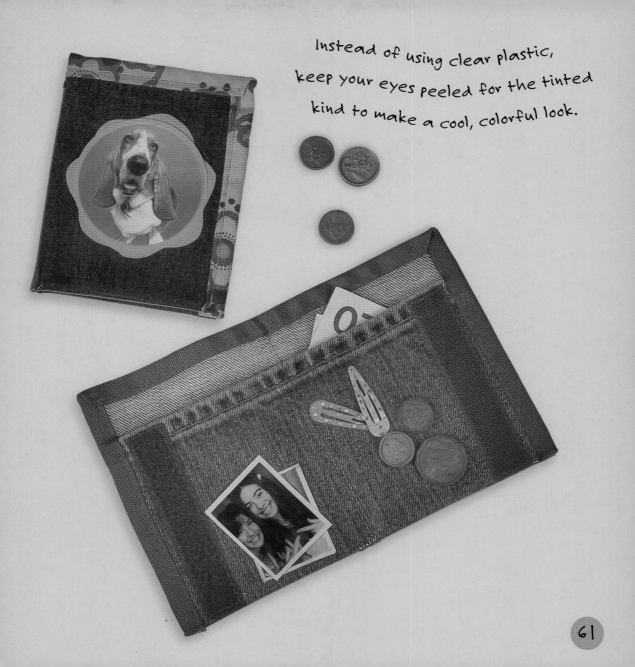

Instead of using clear plastic, keep your eyes peeled for the tinted kind to make a cool, colorful look.

3 Turn the denim over. Use the pencil and ruler to measure and draw a light line up the centre of the fabric. Carefully sew along this line to sew the plastic to the denim. Turn the denim over again. Remove the tape.

4 Start at the hem and stick one side of the Velcro strip 1 cm (1/2 in.) from each side of the wallet edges, as shown. Sew around the edges of both pieces of Velcro.

5 Fold the wallet so the plastic is on the outside and the hemmed edge is 2.5 cm (1 in.) below the other edge.

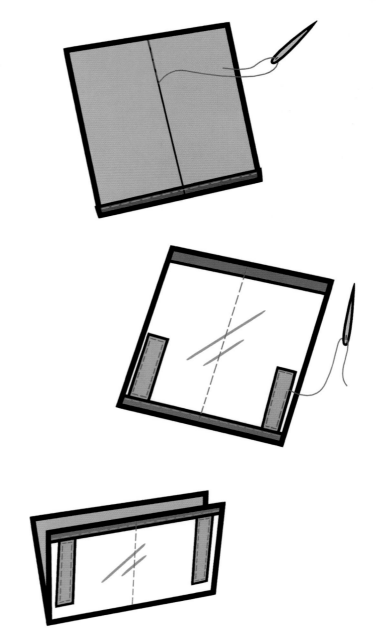

6 Starting at the bottom left corner, pin the ribbon around the three sides to finish at the bottom right corner. (Make sure you pin only the ribbon area — you don't want to make holes in the plastic.) The ribbon should be folded over the wallet edges so it's even on both sides. When you get to the corners, tuck the extra ribbon under. When you get to the last corner, trim and pin the ribbon so there is 2.5 cm (1 in.) to tuck under.

7 Sew along the ribbon edge and remove the pins.

8 Fold the wallet in half, pressing the Velcro together. Ta-da! Something cool and useful.

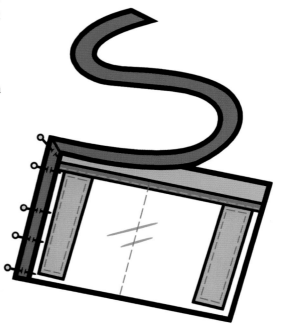

Jean Gem: If you're giving this wallet as a gift, don't forget to put some money in it first — even a penny will do. The money is a good luck charm so your friend will always have money in the wallet.

Cute kerchief

STUFF YOU NEED

- a scrap of denim (the bottom of a jean leg will work)
- 100 cm (40 in.) of 2 cm (3/4 in.) wide ribbon
- thread to match the ribbon
- scissors, pins, a measuring tape

Look sassy and disguise a bad hair day all at once — who could ask for anything more?

1 Measure and cut out a triangle of denim that is 40 cm x 30 cm x 30 cm (16 in. x 12 in. x 12 in.). Cut the denim so a flat-felled side seam runs down the center of the triangle for a fun effect.

2 With WSF, fold over and pin a 1 cm (1/2 in.) hem around all three sides of the triangle. Sew the hem and remove the pins.

3 With RSF, lay the ribbon along the long edge of the triangle so an extra 30 cm (12 in.) extends past each corner. Pin and sew along both ribbon edges. Remove the pins. Now this is a cool cover-up!

Try embroidering a design at the tip of the triangle.

For a glam look,

glue some plastic gems on your wristbands instead of studs.

Rockin' bands

STUFF YOU NEED

- a waistband from a pair of jeans
- studs for fabric
- needle-nose pliers
- thread to match the jeans
- Fray-Stop
- scissors, pins, a measuring tape, a pencil

Who wants wrists dripping with diamonds when you can wear these cool wristbands?

1 Carefully trim any remaining denim from the waistband.

2 Measure around your wrist and add 2.5 cm (1 in.). Divide by two to get the measurement for the next step.

3 Using the measurement from step 2, make a mark from each waistband end. Draw a straight line across and cut off the extra fabric.

4 Lay the pieces RSTOG. Pin and sew a 1 cm (1/2 in.) seam along the cut edges. Remove the pins.

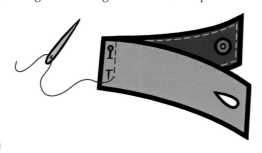

5 One at a time, press the studs into the denim, and use the pliers to press down the stud points on the back. Follow the design shown, or create your own.

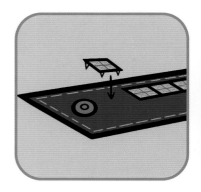

6 Apply Fray-Stop to the cut edges of the wristband. Allow to dry.

Wear Not

Perfectly pleased with your wardrobe but BEYOND BORED with your bedroom? Your clothes have PUNCH but your room's no knockout? Check out this section if you want to:

- [ ] Disguise your JOURNAL with the help of a jean cover.

- [ ] Turn your boring bed into a COMFY LOUNGE for you and your pals.

- [ ] Craft up a footstool, a table and a place to stash your SECRET STUFF ... all at once!

Bottoms-up book cover

STUFF YOU NEED

- a pair of jeans
- a journal, a book, a binder or a scrapbook
- an old belt
- thread to match the jeans
- scissors, pins, a measuring tape, a pencil

Make this cover for your journal to protect your precious thoughts! And you can give your fave book, binder or scrapbook the same treatment, too.

1 Make sure the jeans will fit the book you've chosen by wrapping the back of the waist around the top of the book. The waist should be at least an extra 5 cm (2 in.) wide.

2 Lay the book open flat on the back of the jeans, 1 cm (1/2 in.) from the waist edge. Draw around the book, adding an extra 2.5 cm (1 in.) around. Cut this piece out for the outside cover.

DON'T WORRY if your outfit doesn't have a POCKET 'cause now your binder does.

69

3 Measure all the way around the inside front cover of the book and add an extra 2.5 cm (1 in.) around. Cut two pieces of denim this size from a leg. These are for the insides of the book cover.

4 Pin and sew a 1 cm (¹/₂ in.) hem along one length of each piece from step 3. Remove the pins.

5 Lay the outside cover piece RSF. Lay the two inside pieces on top WSF with the side edges together. Pin in place.

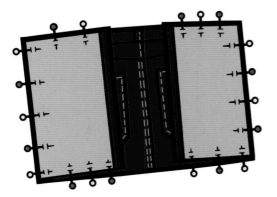

6 Sew the cover pieces together with a 1 cm (¹/₂ in.) seam along the sides and bottom and a 0.5 cm (¹/₄ in.) seam along the top. Remove the pins.

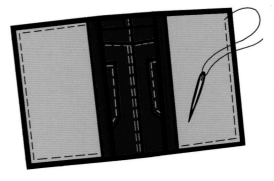

7 Turn the book cover right side out and slide it onto the book. If the cover doesn't fit quite right, cut open the center seam and overlap the edges to fit. Pin and sew the edges in place.

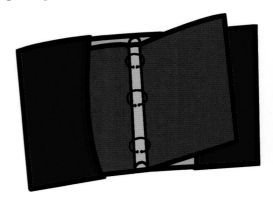

8 Feed the belt through the belt loops. If the belt is too long, trim off the excess. You may have to make more holes in the belt with a leather punch or a hammer and a nail. Ask an adult for help with this, and make sure to hammer on a surface that won't get damaged by the nail.

Jean Gem:

If you're making more than one cover, use an embroidered label or pattern to tell them apart!

Bodacious bolster

A couple of these cozy cushions will turn your bed into a cushy lounging spot for you and your pals. If you have a double bed, sew two bolsters together to make a super long one.

1 Cut off one leg near the top of the jeans. Cut off the bottom hem.

STUFF YOU NEED

- a pair of jeans (straight-legged style works best)
- 1 m (1 yd.) of pom-pom trim
- a package of polyester stuffing
- 2 colored elastic bands
- thread to match the jeans
- scissors, pins, a measuring tape

FORGET the STUFFING and use the bolster to

STASH your PAJAMAS during the day.

2 Turn the leg inside out. Pin and sew a 2.5 cm (1 in.) hem on both ends. Remove the pins.

4 Turn the leg right side out. For both ends, pin the trim around the outside of the hem so the pom-poms face out. Sew along the trim and remove the pins.

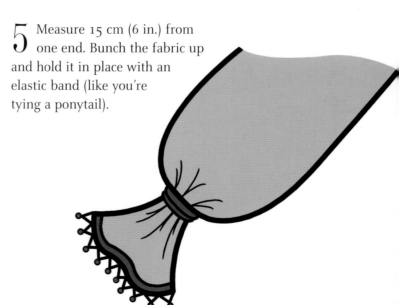

3 Measure across the width of the leg. Double this measurement and add another 2.5 cm (1 in.). Cut two pieces of pom-pom trim this length.

5 Measure 15 cm (6 in.) from one end. Bunch the fabric up and hold it in place with an elastic band (like you're tying a ponytail).

6 Fill the bolster with stuffing until only 15 cm (6 in.) of the leg is empty. Squeeze the bolster as you stuff so that it is not too soft, not too hard, but just right for you. Tie the end with an elastic band like you did in step 5. Toss your bolster on your bed and be divine as you recline.

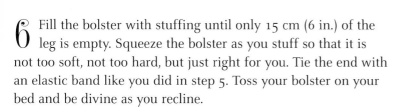

Jean Gem:

Glue on a marabou trim instead of the pom-poms — now it's a boa-dacious bolster!

Fab footstool

STUFF YOU NEED

- 1 m (1 yd.) of denim fabric (washed)
- 30 cm x 30 cm (12 in. x 12 in.) of 2.5 cm (1 in.) foam
- a plastic or wooden crate or sturdy cardboard box, 30 cm x 30 cm x 30 cm (12 in. x 12 in. x 12 in.)
- two pieces of polyester quilt batting: one piece 30 cm x 120 cm (12 in. x 48 in.) and one piece 30 cm x 30 cm (12 in. x 12 in.)
- 1.5 m (1½ yd.) of fleece
- a drinking glass
- a glue gun and glue sticks
- fabric glue
- thread to match the denim
- scissors, pins, a measuring tape, a pencil

Prop up your little piggies on a fabulous footstool. Got friends over? Use it as a low seat or side table. Gotta tidy up first? Hide your junk away underneath.

1 Use the glue gun to glue the piece of foam to the top of the crate. Then glue the smaller piece of batting onto the foam.

2 Working on one side at a time, glue the larger piece of batting around the crate to cover it completely.

You can piece together an old pair of jeans to make this smaller version.

3 Measure and cut two pieces of denim fabric: one that is 33 cm x 33 cm (13 in. x 13 in.) and another that is 33 cm x 125 cm (13 in. x 50 in.). ✳

4 With the RSTOG, fold the larger denim piece in half as shown. Pin the two ends together and sew with a 1 cm (1/2 in.) seam. Remove the pins.

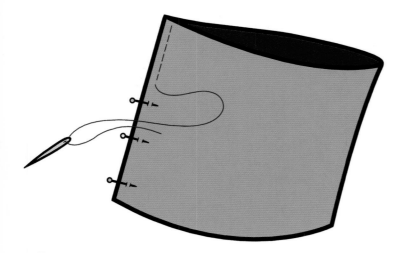

✳ If you're using an old pair of jeans, cut off the legs and open them down the regular side seams. Lay the legs out flat. Pin and sew them together with 1 cm (1/2 in.) seams to make one large piece of material.

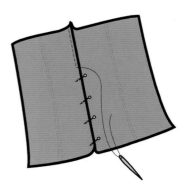

Find a box that's just the right size by wrapping the material around it first. Cut a long piece of material to fit the sides and a square to fit the top. Continue following steps 4 to 8.

5 Lay the square top piece down RSF. Beginning at one corner of the top piece, start with the sewn edge of the side panel and pin it along one edge of the top piece RSTOG. Continue pinning until all four sides of the top piece are attached.

6 Sew around all four sides of the top with a 1 cm (1/2 in.) seam. Remove the pins. Trim any excess fabric off the corners, leaving 1 cm (1/2 in.).

7 Turn the cover right side out and carefully slip it on the crate, making sure the batting stays in place.

8 Turn the crate upside down. Working on one side at a time, glue the edges of the cover inside the crate edges with the glue gun. Pull the cover slightly as you go to keep the material smooth.

9 For the trim, lay the fleece out WSF. Measure and mark 120 cm (48 in.) along the edge. Cut the fleece this length. Take a drinking glass, place it upside down in one corner of the fabric and draw around it. Repeat all along the fabric edge to make a line of touching circles. Cut along the top edges of the circles, going only halfway down and then back up again. You've just made a scalloped edge! Make another one on the other side of the fleece.

10 Using fabric glue, attach the fleece trim along the bottom and top edges of the footstool as shown. Use a few pins to hold it in place while it dries. Remove the pins. Now you can put up your feet and relax. You deserve it!

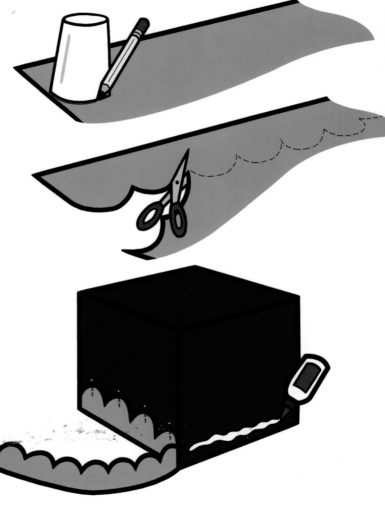